How to Start a Financially Successful Daycare:
A step by step guide to starting your own daycare

Corey Parchman

www.coreyparchman.com

Copyright © 2019 Corey Parchman

All rights reserved.

www.coreyparchman.com

DEDICATION

In everyone's lives there are those whose light has shined brighter and warmer than others. For me, that was my grandmother, Inez Wynn. For all those times and all the advice, for giving me words of encouragement when I needed it….and most of all for helping me to understand my place in the world, this book , and my life, is a legacy to her love.

www.coreyparchman.com

CONTENTS

	Acknowledgments	i
1	Know Why You Want To Do This	3
2	Choose Your School Type	8
3	Doing Business As….	19
4	Making it Legal	24
5	Zoning and Regulations	28
6	Hiring Employees	33
7	Getting the Word Out	40
8	The Parent Handbook	46
9	The Staff Handbook	50
10	Selecting Curriculum	56
11	Accreditation	62
12	Setting a Sustainable Pricing Structure	67

www.coreyparchman.com

ACKNOWLEDGMENTS

There are a number of people that have helped to make this book a reality. First, I'd like to thank my dad, Edward Parchman, who taught me to push through and aim high. Also, I have to acknowledge my 4th grade teacher, Mrs. Edna May, who never told me I couldn't achieve something. It is her love of children and a desire to see them succeed that has inspired me to develop schools to reach those often overlooked, forgotten or passed over children…especially those little men who don't always have a voice that can be heard

INTRODUCTION

I've had many titles over the years: NFL wide receiver, philanthropist, business owner. And while those are all great titles, and ones that I am proud to own, most people are unfamiliar with my other title: educator. Most remember me from the NFL or, setting records at Ball State. But some of the most meaningful work that I've done has come from being able to use my degree in which I received from Ball State. Even while I was pursuing other avenues after my NFL career, my passion for helping and working with children never left me. Finally, I was able to realize a personal goal of mine: to bring positive role models (both men and women) to children living in difficult situations. Having lost my own dad when I was just 9, I get it. I know what kids can face when it's just them and their mother trying to make it. Luckily for me I also had some incredible teachers and a grandmother who stepped up to help me succeed. In large part, this is my way of paying them back and paying it forward.

Having been at this for a while now, I can tell you that after so many people asking me how I've done what I've done with the daycare business, I decided to put all of my experience into a one-stop-shop book. When I was starting there wasn't just one place to go for all of the information that I needed. What sort of licenses did I need? Where would I find teachers? How did I even begin to know how to meet state rules regarding finding a building to have the daycare in?!! I've saved you that time and trouble and I guarantee if you'll trust the process, you'll not only create a business that has the potential to change people's lives, but you'll change yours in the process.

This book will help you plan, prepare and operate a successful Home Daycare or Daycare Center. I'll walk you step by step through all of it, from how to start, operate, and grow your center. At the end of each chapter, I'll also give you additional resources or things to think about that can help you continue your education and to help you critically think about the process. If you have a passion for working with children. If you want to create a profession where you aren't living paycheck to paycheck, then starting a Daycare will be a win/win situation for everyone. I'm extremely humbled and grateful that you're taking the time to read the material in this book. Here's to your success, and the success of every student you serve.

Corey Parchman

CHAPTER ONE
Know Why You Want To Do This

If everyone could own and run a daycare there'd be more successful ones out there. If you aren't ready to spend some long days and nights, and at the minimum 10-14 hour days, then you may not be motivated enough to make something like this work. It takes time to get the process and foundations laid for a successful school, and in no small part is the fact that you MUST be a people person. You will find yourself having to deal with parents, staff and state officials.

Secondly, are you an organized person? Most businesses will require you to be organized, but I'm telling you that in a daycare organization has GOT to be a part of the operation, and a part of who you are as the founder. Saving time and avoiding stress are some of the payoffs for being organized.

Next, are you someone that can make decisions, even the hard choices when it comes to it? Take a minute a look back over your life up until this point. Who has been the big decision maker in your life? How did you handle it when you made a decision and it turned out to be the wrong one? It will happen you know. Preparation and planning is one of the most crucial components of this industry. Trust me, I know.

How are you as far as marketing and getting the word out? If you don't have a background in marketing or sales, you will need to use some of the information in this book to get you started. But in the end, it is a constant and ongoing task and if you do not enjoy that, you'll have to plan to bring someone on to do it for you. And most of them, even if they are related to you, won't do it for free (not for long anyway).

Now, I'm not going to tell you that you will start making money hands over fists right off the bat. It's not like a "Reality Show" you're up in going in 30 minutes. You have to be prepared to have some tight financial days at first. But, I can also tell you that if you trust the process and surround yourself with the right people in the right places, you will not only survive the early times, you will thrive and do well.

The Numbers Don't Lie

Regardless of the economy the daycare business has continued to grow at a steady pace. Last year along, the revenue in the child services sector had a gain of 4%, which put it at over $33.6 billion dollars. This industry created over 1.5 million jobs and there were more than 120,000 licensed centers.

Take a minute to create a list, or spreadsheet, of your competition in the area. How many daycares are there already? How many kids go there? You can find this out by simply walking in and asking for a tour of the competition's facility. Now, ask yourself the hard question: how will yours be any different? For me, the answer to that was I wanted to create a daycare academy for young boys. For me, working with young daycare boys has allowed us to create a safe atmosphere where they can learn how to express themselves in a constructive and caring way, instead of being physical or venting their frustration negatively. You've got to figure out what will make your daycare different than the rest, otherwise you're going to be starting off at a disadvantage against centers that have been in business longer.

Starting a daycare may be a good idea for you if you:
- Love working with kids and families.
- Like seeing children learn and succeed.
- Are in pretty good health and can work long hours.
- Can handle financial slumps initially.
- Don't mind putting in the time to learn and plan.

I've owned, and still do, a lot of different businesses, and I can tell you that there's a lot of crossover when it comes to creating a business that involves children. But that's where the comparison ends. In many businesses the product is something you've made, or it's a service that you offer, like cutting someone's grass. When your product and service involves people, especially very young children, a one-size-fits-all business model won't work. Unlike regular businesses, you will have to not only do the basic business processes, but you'll also have to meet state and federal guidelines, select curriculum to use, make sure that your teachers continue to receive training, and much more. You should go into the daycare business with your eyes wide open and determine that when an obstacle presents itself, you go around it or through it (something my NFL career taught me about over and over).

Extra Financial Help and Where to Find It

Believe it or not, depending on how you structure your business, your daycare or daycare may be eligible for various grants and subsidies from the local, state and federal government. This is especially true if you are placing your school in an area that is considered "socially and economically challenged". That's a ten dollar phrase for poverty. Situating your school where there aren't a lot of schools because it is in an area of town that is rough can be a win/win situation, not only for the kids and their families who will benefit, but in the money that most governmental offices are willing to give to those willing to do that. Everything from free or subsidized food to offering free VPK funding is possible. Each state has their own different approach. I had already planned to set up my school on the eastside of Indianapolis, because that's where I knew the kind of help I wanted to offer would have the most impact. In fact, when I first decided to situate my academy on the eastside, I had no idea that there were other sources of income that I might qualify for. It pays to look around and ask. If this is not something you want to do or feel compelled to do, then either get someone to do it for you, or possibly rethink why it is you want to open up a daycare business.

Can You Wear Many Hats?

I love the fast-paced nature of this business, but it isn't for everyone. From organizing the business to getting the word out, I wore all of the hats that were necessary for making the center successful. The benefit of wearing all of the hats at least once is that you understand what it takes to do that particular job and you'll be able to tell quickly if someone isn't doing it right. When you start up a daycare or daycare you may be called upon to be not only a business person, but an educator, employer, salesperson as well as the custodian and cook. It may all fall to you at first as you build up your clientele.

In the end, you know yourself better than anyone else. Having the very frank conversation with yourself before starting down this road is the only way to know what your motivation for doing this is. There's no test, no accountability to another person at this stage of the game. Just you and the idea of starting a business for children.

For me, it has all been worth it and among all of my life's accomplishments it stands as one of those that I'm most proud of. That could be your story, too.

If I haven't scared you away and you are determined to move forward, you will have my promise that you're not going to do it alone. This book can really move you from where you are to where you want to be, as long as you take the advice as it is given and work hard to meet the goals as they're set for you. In the NFL professional players use a playbook. This playbook is carefully guarded because in it are all of our special plays, strategies and goals. I'm offering you my "playbook" for getting a daycare or daycare off and running. So if you're ready….huddle up….

CHAPTER TWO

Choose Your School Type

There are many types of childcare out there. Depending on what state you are in, there may be as many as six or seven different categories. The main distinction between them all is how you plan to offer childcare and what you plan to offer children by way of education. This chapter will focus on giving you the information so you can make a educated decision about which type of childcare you want to offer. In my state, which is Indiana, you can offer a home based childcare or a center based. If you plan to have no more than five or six kids in your home and you charge for keeping the children, then you would be considered a homebased childcare business.

However, if you'd like to offer care to more than five or six children, and increase the age range, then you would be considered a center-based childcare business. That's pretty much true regardless of where you set up shop. Look at your state's licensing agency and see what the requirements are for:

- Number of children per square foot.
- Inspections required.
- Licensing required.
- Training required.
- Teacher to student ratios.
- Building or home requirements.

children leave the daycare to begin their formal academic education, they are fully ready with some basic skills that will contribute to their early success at school. Having said that, many childcare centers also offer a daycare within the larger context of the childcare center. You must decide which you would rather do and the services you see yourself offering. Daycares will have a few more inspections and the curriculum and teachers will be periodically required to continue their education as well as renew their early childhood licensing.

A study conducted observed the data produced by children who had attended a HeadStart program versus those who did not. The study conducted by the Brookings Institute, confirmed that center-based daycares, compared to home-based care, saw vast differences between those children developmentally, particularly in the area of vocabulary and communication skills. But that produces the entire question of access, doesn't it? What about families who don't have access to publicly funded daycare programs? What about those who cannot afford private daycare programs? Researchers stated that the main takeaway from this study was that the home based programs needed to step up their offerings to match their center-based contemporaries.

Now I'm not trying to talk you out of starting a home based childcare or daycare in your home. All I'm saying is that if you opt to go that route you will want to give the kids you take care of all of the advantages so they are ready for school like the rest.

Advantages of Home Based Childcare/Daycare

There are a lot of reasons why it can be a good idea to start out as a home based childcare business, and then later expand to a center based business. Here is a quick list of the advantages, followed by some of the drawbacks you should consider.

1. Low startup cost and overhead. You won't have a rental fee for the space, and you won't have a separate utility bill.
2. Tax deductions will benefit you at a higher rate. For example, you can take deductions for portions of the mortgage payment, utilities, and more.
3. It does not take as long to launch your business. You can literally be ready to go in just a few months' time.
4. Parents love smaller classroom sizes and individualized attention for their children. Larger center-based schools don't always have the luxury of that one-on-one that many home-based childcare centers can offer.
5. There are often fewer cases of illness because the children are exposed to less classmates.
6. You can be more flexible and accommodating for parents than larger centers.
7. You can offer lower tuition rates than most center based childcare centers.

Disadvantages of Home Based Childcare/Daycare

1. There will be wear and tear on your house.
2. Your own personal space is going to be limited.
3. You can only handle so many children in your house by law, and the age of those children may also be restricted.
4. Often the level of education by the caregivers is less than at a center-based facility.
5. Children may be exposed more often to high television viewing than children in a center-based childcare situation.
6. There is often no additional staff, so if you are sick, the children have to find somewhere else to go, or you have to get a trusted substitute.

Advantages of a Center Based Childcare/Daycare

Center-based child care centers simply mean that you are offering child care and daycare services in a larger space, for more children. Often this works out well especially if you are in an area that does not already have a lot of other daycare centers. Some of the distinct advantages of a center based childcare or daycare situation include:

1. Have better trained/educated teachers (though this is not always a guarantee…certain states may vary).
2. Structured schedule, more school-like, which gives older children an advantage when they start formal education.

3. The curriculum is usually richer with more extra curricular activities being possible. These can include everything from field trips to offering foreign language classes.
4. Technology is often more prevalent in center-based schools than in a home center.
5. Security is tighter and often includes secured entrances, and often include in-class video cameras for parents to check in on their children.
6. Are trained to spot developmental problems early so parents can enact some early intervention before children start kindergarten.
7. Can take in many more children, which means much more potential for revenue.

Disadvantages of a Center Based Childcare/Daycare

1. Depending on the center, there could be high staff turnover rates which impact young children.
2. Policies and procedures do not have a lot of flexibility.
3. Higher tuition rates, as a general rule.
4. Operating and startup costs are higher.
5. Must meet state rules and regulations and prepare for inspections more often than home based childcare.
6. Have more paperwork to keep up with.
7. Must provide approved and appropriate curriculum.

A Word About Voluntary Daycare Programs

In Indiana, our voluntary daycare program is called the ON MY Way Pre-K program. In your state, it may be called something else. The program is for four year old children and its aim is to provide the skills and education necessary to prepare children for kindergarten. Not all childcare centers or homebased situations are allowed to participate. Most pre-k programs like On My Way and the Headstart programs require your business to be a licensed childcare facility and be accredited by a recognized accrediting association. If your childcare business is a level 3 or better Path to Quality then you qualify. The advantage for offering the program is that many parents will specifically seek out situations such as voluntary daycare programs for their children. In some states you can receive additional funding for children you take into the voluntary pre-k program who are from identified socio-economically depressed areas and whose residents are considered academically "at risk".

Franchises, Existing Businesses Branches and Startups

Another consideration you might want to look at is going with a readymade franchise childcare center. The advantages in going with a franchise is that the business plan, the marketing materials, much of the planning and strategies have already been done for you. This can give you a giant leap ahead when it comes to getting your business started. Many will also mentor you through the first year or so, answering questions you may have.

The drawback with a franchise is that most want a percentage of your earnings in return for their help. This payment to the parent company may last as long as you continue to do business under their name. And, many of them will have you sign, along with many other documents, a non-compete clause which means that if you decide you want to start up your own childcare facility you are limited as to where you can do that, or if you can do that at all.
It can be a good way to get your start and have a safety net, but it does come at a literal and figurative price.

For one reason or another owners of childcare businesses may decide they want to get out of the industry or they are planning to retire. This can be an excellent opportunity to get a building that is already equipped for children, already has the approval from the state, and has a built-in clientele. Many times, the owners of such businesses are willing to work out owner-financing options, or other creative financing to help you continue the work they started. Look for these opportunities in the real estate for sale section in your town. Or use the keywords "educational business for sale" or "daycare centers for sale". Most are highly motivated to sell.

If you have not ever run a business before and are wondering if you can make a go of it yourself, you might want to try your hand at running a branch center for an already established childcare company. This is different from a franchise in that you don't own the building or the business, but are the manager of the operation. This gives you a steady paycheck while you learn what it takes to own and run your own center.

Look for larger daycares in the area and then speak with the owner about opening up another branch of their business in a great location you have in mind. They may already have one, in which case you are set.

Last, you can startup your own business from the ground up. This option does give you the greatest amount of freedom as far as designing the program exactly as you'd like to see it. You can put your fingerprint on the business from day one, and the systems and processes you put in place are no one else's but yours. You will have the most control over the curriculum, selection of the staff, creation of your brand, and the design of the rooms and the building.

Know the Basics of Childcare Regulation

When trying to make up your mind about which type of childcare or daycare situation you want to offer, consider that you will need to meet certain basic requirements, regardless of which state you operate in. Many of those designations have to do with the terminology regarding the age of the children in your care, as well as how many caregivers and space requirements are necessary to remain compliant. Here is a general overview, but please make sure to look it up through your stare's childcare licensing bureau.

Infants and Toddlers

If you are planning to provide care for infants, age 6 weeks to 11 months of age, then you will need to make sure you meet the ratio of caregivers to infants. In most states this number is quite small. In Indiana it is a 4:1 ratio (four children to one caregiver), but in your state it could be fewer than that. Toddlers are children that are 1-2 years of age, and the ratios are approximately 5:1. Most centers have more than one teacher in a classroom to meet these requirements. It is also a safety issue, which is why most states are very strict about these numbers.

Daycare (Ages 3-4)

The ratios for these classes are approximately 10:1 or 12:1. In Indiana, for example, it is common to see three and four year olds mixed in together in a pre-k classroom. Therefore, the ratios are based on the youngest kid in the class. Check your state listings to be sure.

Daycare (Ages 4-5)

Children in this group are older four year olds and five year olds who were not yet old enough or ready for kindergarten. These children will be your most active, inquisitive, and I've got to tell you, they are just plain fun! They are interested in learning anything you show them and this is where you can really set some great foundations for future learning situations.

Other Services and Ways to Create Revenue

When you consider what your childcare or daycare will look like, and what it will offer, you can also offer parents additional value services. Services such as afterschool care, holiday camps, part time care, drop in care, or summer camps are just some of the possibilities. Some centers also offer recreational and extra-curricular activities for afterschool children, such as field trips, homework help, music. lessons or sports. All of it is benefiting children in your area, as well as their families, and it is another line of revenue for you.

Drop-In Care, Part-Time Care and Extended Hours Care

Depending on where your center is located, you may want to offer parents the option of dropping their children off at any time to be cared for while they take care of errands, go to medical appointments, or attend a job interview. Having the space to take in children at a moment's notice can also boost your bottom line and it is a great service to families who may not be able to afford a full time care situation, but can definitely utilize the service as needed.

Parents who work the late shift, or whose work hours mean they have to pick up their children after typical evening hours will gravitate toward those situations where their workhour needs are met. Centers and homebased childcare businesses who can offer extended hours, or even just part-time care can be a win/win situation for everyone involved. In many instances, when circumstances improve they will bring their child to your center on a full time basis.

Things to Think About

Get yourself a notebook, or create a spreadsheet on your computer and begin answering the following questions for yourself:

1. What does my daycare childcare center or daycare look like in my mind's eye? Is it a center or home based operation?
2. If it is center based, where are some good locations?
3. Who are the current daycares or childcare companies in the immediate area?
4. How will your childcare business be any different from the others?
5. What does your city require as far as business licensing? What does your state require?
6. What is your state's ratios for caregiver/teacher to child (by age)?
7. Which age group will you offer care to?
8. Will you offer additional services beyond childcare/daycare? If so, what?
9. If you are offering home-based care, where in your home will you keep the children and how many, based on state regulations, can you realistically keep?
10. What insurance does your state require you to have?

This is an important first step in moving toward your goal of owning and running a daycare for a living. Taking the time to plan is crucial to your success. In the next chapters we'll discuss some of this in more detail, such as how to set your rates and collect fees, develop policies and procedures, and how to find good staff. Don't go on to the next chapter until you've done your homework above. As Coach Tony Dungy of the Indianapolis Colts and Tampa Bay Buccaneers once told me, "There are no shortcuts to glory."

CHAPTER THREE
Doing Business As….

Now that you've chosen the type of childcare business you are interested in opening, you'll still have a number of legal hoops to jump through. I've taken the time to place them in easy to reference sections so that they are easy to find later when you need to look back at them. Believe me, you will reference them for a while until you've determined which structure is right for you, which gives you and your business the most tax advantages and wage protection, and how much paperwork is involved with each business structure. There are many business structures out there, but most people stick to the big five: Sole Proprietorships, Limited Liability Partnerships, Limited Liability Corporations, S-Corporations and Corporations. There are permutations of each of these, but these are the most popular choices. Not all of them are created equally, either, when it comes to what each will allow you to do in regard to tax deductions, hiring employees and insurance requirements. Take the time to review each of these structures, speak with an accountant you trust for some backup advice, and then make a choice. **I'll tell you right now, I'm not an accountant or a lawyer, so getting the advice of a good accountant and lawyer that knows small businesses is another very good thing you can do for yourself.** The good news is…you can get a do-over if you choose a structure and you decide it's not working for you.

Sole Proprietorships

As the name suggests you are listed as the sole owner and operator of the business. At first blush it may seem like this is the one for you, and it might be, but don't assume just because it matches your current circumstance that you should stop considering the other possible structures. Here's the quick 411 on Sole Proprietorships:

Pros and Cons for Sole Proprietorships

Pros	Simple paperwork to submit.	Do not have to share business with anyone.	Management flexibility.	You own all of the assets in the business.	Less government oversight.	Less recordkeeping compared to other structures.	
Cons	Taxed at highest rate of all business structures.	Personal assets are not protected in case of a lawsuit.	You assume all of the liability.	Harder to raise financing from banks.	Cannot issue stocks.	Has a harder time expanding.	

Limited Liability Partnerships

This business type is primarily for those who want to work with a partner to open their daycare. This means that you will share the profits and losses as well as the managerial duties. This structure has the distinct advantage over the sole proprietorship in that it protects your personal income in case of a law suit. But there are also some drawbacks, too.

Pros and Cons for Limited Liability Partnerships

Pros	Partners are shielded from each others misconduct.	Capital investments are possible.	Personal assets are protected.	
Cons	Some states won't allow LLPs at all.	Profits are passed through to the partners who pay taxes based on their own tax bracket.	You have a partner to consider when making decisions.	Harder to dissolve if you want to close the business down.

Limited Liability Corporations(LLC)

When you are just starting out it can be hard to see yourself as a corporation. However, you may want to reconsider. A Limited Liability Corporation (LLC) is a business structure that takes the best from a sole proprietorship with the tax advantages and personal income protection qualities of the Limited Liability Partnership.

Pros and Cons for Limited Liability Corporations

Pros	You can be a sole operator or have partners.	The business is not taxed on the profits.	Personal assets are protected	Greater number of tax deductions available.
Cons	More paperwork to fill out.	Profits are passed through to the owner who pays taxes based on their own tax bracket.	If the situation is severe enough, judges can dissolve the protection afforded by the LLC if you have not kept your personal and business assets separate.	Harder to dissolve if you want to close the business down.

S-Corporations

When it comes to realizing the best of all worlds, many savvy businesses opt for the S-Corporation. This gives you increased protection for your personal assets, offers you many more tax benefits, and allows you to have employees. This structure allows you to expand in the future without having to restructure your business.

Pros	You can be a sole operator or have partners.	The business is not taxed on the profits.	Personal assets are protected	Greater number of tax deductions available.
Cons	More paperwork to fill out.	Profits are passed through to the owner who pays taxes based on their own tax bracket.	Much more record keeping necessary	You have to submit an annual report and in some states show that you hold regular shareholder meetings.

Corporations

As with the S-Corporation, there are a number of advantages that will open up for you with this business structure. You will have the most deductions allowed come tax time, you assume zero liability for the businesses debts. This structure allows you to create branches in the future and even sell stock if you so choose.

Pros	You can be a sole operator or have partners.	You can receive both a salary and a dividend as a shareholder.	Personal assets are protected	Greater number of tax deductions available.
Cons	More paperwork to fill out.	You could be subject to double taxation in your state.	Much more record keeping necessary	Are most often flagged for audit by the IRS.

Choosing the right structure for your business can make your life easier or more difficult depending on how you handle it. As a general rule, I would advise against the sole proprietorship because you are taxed at a higher rate and you are still on the hook if something happens and your business is sued. In these cases you are just one lawsuit away from having to close your doors. It is just not worth the risk. Still, if you are opening a home based childcare situation, then a sole proprietorship may be something you want to do as you know your clients and don't think a lawsuit is likely. Personally, I don't like to play the odds.

S-Corporations and LLCs, if your state allows them, seem to be the best vehicle for childcare and daycares. They allow for greater flexibility, hiring of employees, and in the case of the S-Corporation give you a couple of ways to increase your revenue. Plus, the tax deductions you can take are stellar compared to the other structures.

What will it cost? Most states will have an online platform that you can use to file your paperwork for a business entity. Just make sure that it is the OFFICIAL site as there are a lot of copycat sites out there that look legit and they're just scammers, or they are independent agents that submit the paperwork for you. You can fill this out easily enough by yourself. Save your startup money for other expenses. Each state will charge a different amount to file your paperwork, but generally speaking you can estimate between $100-300 dollars. Once you file it, you only have to renew it once a year and you're good. Once again I'm not an attorney or accountant I would advise seeking professional council these are simply suggestions.

Things to Think About
1. Do you have partners you plan to operate the business with?
2. What are your state's laws in regard to the various structures?
3. Which structures are recognized by your state?
4. How organized can you be with maintaining records?

CHAPTER FOUR
Making it Legal

Depending on where you live in the U.S. there will be additional state and local licenses and permits that you will have to get. Laws vary from one state to the next, but are generally the same for daycares and daycares. The first place to find this information is to call the local Department of Child Welfare, or the Human Services department. The following section lays the most typical types of licenses needed in order to open your doors. As with anything legal make sure you are surrounding yourself with people in the know. I'm providing the information to point you in the right direction, but remember, I'm not a lawyer or an accountant.

Business Name Registration

You may think you have the most clever and unique name, only to go and register it and find out that it is already taken and you can't use it. I've heard so many nightmare tales of daycare owners going ahead and having their logo, website and business cards already printed up only to find out when they go to register than they've wasted their money. Hold off on that fun stuff and find out if you can actually call your business what you want to. Your state's Department of Labor will usually have a tab just for businesses looking to start in the state. In that section you will see a place to see if your name is available. Some states let you reserve that name until you finish the rest of your paperwork so that no one comes in behind you and takes the name.

Business Bank Account

In order to protect your assets, as much as possible, you should open up a separate bank account for your business. This will be the account that you use to pay employees, send off payroll taxes and take care of purchasing supplies and services for the business. Do not be tempted to withdraw money out of this account for personal uses, ever. It could come back on you depending on which business structure you've decided on. You may want to have the bank create a special set of checks for you to use, or there are various programs you can get that will print payroll checks right from your computer.

Local and State Business Registration

Each city and township has its own rules about who needs a business license. Guaranteed a daycare or daycare will be one of them. Call your county clerk's office and ask. In many jurisdictions you also have to have a background check for both criminal and sexual offender databases. Some require that the owner of the daycare have a degree in an education-related field. Don't let that stop you, though. All you have to do is hire a director who DOES have that background and in most states you'll have met the requirement. Yes, in most states you will be required to have a license even if you are running the business from your home. You should also check with your Home Owners Association because they may not allow you to run the business using your home.

Daycare or Child Care Licensing

If you are unsure where your local licensing offices are, there are many free services that will look that information up for you. One that is nationwide is the childcareaware.org group. Simply plug in your zip code and they'll tell you where the office is located, along with contact information. These offices may also have contacts for startup financing and information specific to your area. Child care licensing is a separate license from the business license. You can find the state specific requirements using the site Childcare Aware.

Insurance Requirements

You are going to need liability insurance. Some states specify the minimum amount that you have to have, while others leave it up to you. Most recommend at least a million dollar general liability policy. Usually, these cost approximately $300 a year, but can vary from one state to the next. You can find this type of insurance from your regular insurance agent who handles your home and auto insurance.

Taxes

There is much you will need to learn about the taxes involved with running a business with numerous employees. The two you will need to be aware of in particular are payroll taxes and quarterly taxes. Both of these types of taxes should be paid on time without fail. Here's a short tutorial on what these two types of taxes are. Again, I am far from being an accountant and I would urge you find a good one before you even open your doors. But, understanding a little bit about it before you go to me with him or her is never a bad idea.

Payroll Taxes

You've experienced payroll taxes yourself if you've ever worked for anyone else. This is the amount of money that is withheld from your paycheck each time. Each state handles how they require payroll taxes to be paid so you will have to speak to your accountant about that. Additionally, there are rules and regulations surrounding those states that don't impose an income tax. Both employers and employees is most states will contribute a portion of the money made in a given time period to payroll taxes.

Quarterly Taxes

This was one of the most confusing taxes to me when I first started. Luckily I had someone to give me some good advice and explain it to me. Basically, the IRS wants to know what you "think" your income is going to be for the coming year. It really is a "best guess" on your part. Based on that number you will make quarterly payments (four times a year) of taxes on that presumed amount. If you see that your best guess needs to be adjusted there are ways to do that, too. How much will you pay in taxes? That is all based on your estimation of income for your first year. Your accountant can help you arrive at a beginning figure.

Things to Think About
1. Where is your local business licensing office?
2. What are the costs for filing for the various licenses you require?
3. What is the name of your business going to be and is it available?
4. How much insurance does your agent and the child care offices suggest you carry? How much is it?
5. Who are some accountants in my area who specialize in small businesses? Do I have a branch of the SBA (Small Business Association) in my area and if so, where are they located?

CHAPTER FIVE
Zoning and Regulations

As with a lot of things, location matters. You will want to pick a location that is close to a main street, that has easy access and plenty of parking. Having a street front also makes your center visible to those who drive past it everyday. One of the first places to look is online. Stick a keyword search in for commercial properties for sale, or childcare centers for sale. If you are lucky and find a building that has already had a former childcare center, then you will fasttrack through a lot of the process.

However, most of you will be starting from the ground up. Narrow down your search to a few buildings that look like good candidates, then give them a tour. Select buildings that are in areas where there are lots of families and children. How do you find out this info? Go onto real estate websites (Loopnet is a good one) and they'll have a lot of free demographic data on an area. For example, suppose you do your research on one of the properties and learn that there are approximately 4,000 kids living in the area that are under the age of five, and there's only one daycare within a 10-20 mile radius. That's golden.

Develop a Pay Model

When it comes to finding a good location you have to figure into that your pay model. This is the model you will use to charge parents. If you are going to private pay only, where parents pay you for the service and you don't accept subsidies, then you'll want to situate yourself in a higher income area where parents can afford to do private pay. However, your best bet if you want to increase your earnings is to accept both types of payments. Middle income areas usually have a mixture of private pay and subsidies.

Buy or Lease?

The best advice I can give you on this is to lease the building until you are 100% sure it is where you want to be. Here are some things to think about concerning this. For example, supposed you received funding to buy a $100,000 building and you're going to put $20,000 down on it. You will be responsible for the upkeep and maintenance on the building just as if you were renting it. You are still paying taxes, getting insurance and all of the other costs associated with getting started. Leasing is your best bet.

Licensing Standards for Your Building

Your state will have specific guidelines for the location of a daycare. For example, in some states the daycare center cannot be located within a certain radius of a liquor store. Still others require that the building have a drop off area in the front of the building that is safe. The only way to find out what all of the regulations are for your area is to contact your state childcare licensing offices or websites. There is usually a checklist for purchasing or renting a building that you can use when you are considering a place to run your business from.

Getting in the Zone

You will have to know the zone for the building you are interested in. The realtor or the leasing agent can give you this information. This zone listing will tell you what kind of use the property qualifies for. Just to be sure, take the zoning designation to your childcare licensing agency and ask if the way the building is zoned is okay for use as a center. Many requirements also state that you have to have adequate parking. If your center is in a largely urban area this requirement may be waived.

The worst case scenario is to get moved in or start work on the center only to find out that the state requires you to have parking and you don't have any room to add parking. You're stuck! Playground area is also important. Most states require there to be some area adjacent to the center where children can play safely.

Kitchens, Washrooms and Fountains

The daycare kitchen will have different requirements than from a regular home kitchen. Certain states require your sink to have three compartments and grease traps. Some require that you have a commercial hood and that the hot water be kept at a certain temperature. This will be listed out on that checklist issued by the state. There are also certain guidelines for centers that have washers and dryers on the premises. Some states require that there be water fountains installed in the building for children to use, so pay attention to this requirement and if it is required make sure that the building you are considering has the room for them. Restrooms are also regulated. You will need to have so many bathrooms per so many students. For example, your state may list that there has to be one bathroom of you have ten or less students.

Space…the Final Frontier

The building you are considering has to have the right amount of space. Your state will specify how much square feet must be given to each child in your care. Generally speaking, the younger the child the greater the space required. Where I am it's 35 square feet per kid up to 20 kids for 4-5 year olds. So, that means that I have to have at least 1,400 square feet of usable space in the classroom.

You can consider that at least 25% or that will be non-usable space because it is covered with bookshelves, sinks or furniture. A good rule of thumb is to overestimate your square footage needs by at least 25%.

Teacher to Student Ratios

Consider that the state will also regulate how many children can be left with a single adult to care for them. The younger the child the lower the number of children to teacher ratio. In most states infants are at a four to one ratio (four babies to one caregiver). The number of children to teacher ratio increases as the children go up in age. So, while you are in your planning stages you will need to predict which rooms in your potential building will house which age groups and what the potential for expansion is.

A typical setup could be the following:

	2- Two year old classes: 8 children per classroom/2 teachers required	2-Three year old classes: 12 per classroom/2 teachers required	3-Four year old classes: 16 per classroom/2 teachers required	One Pre-K Class: 20 per classroom 2 teachers required
35 SQ FT per child	560 square feet (approximately a 25 x 25 room, or 280 sq ft per classroom)	840 square feet (approximately a 30 x 30 room or 420 sq ft per classroom))	1680 square feet (approximately a 42 x 42 room, or 560 sq ft per classroom)	700 square feet needed.
Teacher to Student Ratio	1:4	1:6	1:8	1:10

These numbers are just used for illustration. You will have to locate the childcare handbook for your state to get the correct ratios and numbers to plug in. However, you should create your own chart just like the above so that you know how big each room needs to be before you start looking at buildings. The National Association for the Education of Young Children (NAEYC) also has a standardized chart that you can use, too. It is available online. It might be the case that when you first open your doors you don't have enough kids for each age group to have their own room. Most states allow children of a similar age to be mixed together. In mixed age group rooms most states also have guidelines concerning the space needed and teacher ratios required.

Keep in mind that there will also be rules governing older children who you may keep in an afterschool program so you have to figure in the space for them as well.

Things to Think About:
- Create a chart or spreadsheet for locations that meet your demographic needs (are there enough children in that area and how many?)
- In the areas you have identified, how many childcare centers are there already?
- What are the requirements of your state for number of children per classroom, per age?
- How many caregivers or teachers are required by state law?
- What will your pricing model be (private pay, subsidies, or both)?
- How much square footage will you need for your projected first year in business?

CHAPTER SIX
Hiring Employees

Who you will hire will make a huge impact on the success of your daycare and childcare center. For each employee you will be required to keep a file that will include a wide range of information including a current physical, background check and more. Keeping everything current with employees, knowing where to find good employees, how to interview them and select those who are not only very good at what they do, but are individuals that you believe you would work well with is crucial to your success. Children do not take to change well and they often form bonds with their teachers. Having teachers come and go constantly during the course of a school year can be traumatic to young children. Unhappy children equal unhappy parents. You do not want to go there.

Finding Quality Employees

It used to be that you could just place an ad in the paper and get a good response rate. Now, of course, that's no longer true. In fact, I would say that placing an ad in the paper is a gigantic waste of your time and it is expensive, too. You will get mixed results on such sites as CareerBuilder, Monster or even Craigslist. What I've found on those sites is that you have to sift through thousands of submitted resumes that it's a monumental task.

One of the best ways to find the right employees is to simply ask for referrals from people you might already know. Advertise at local colleges, too, as many students who are graduating will be looking for a job. Do a quick internet search and see if there are job fairs where you can set up a booth, and use your social media, church and community bulletin boards, and even talk with local school placement agencies to let them know you are looking to hire.

One of the key aspects to finding and keeping good teachers is to offer them a fair wage, benefits and the chance to grow professionally. What is a fair wage? Current rates list the average childcare working making $9.40 an hour with benefits. Daycare teachers are paid more than that, and they should be because they require more training and have to keep their credentials current. The Bureau of Labor Statistics state that daycare teachers typically earn $12.64 an hour with benefits. Daycare administrators make from $19.36 to $21.68 an hour. Knowing these numbers ahead of time can help you to calculate what type of operating capital you are going to need in order to open your doors.

To weed out those who are not serious about the position, make sure that the application process takes some time to complete. Ask for a detailed cover letter, resume and professional references. Those who cannot follow directions can be discarded. I would suggest that you interview way more individuals than you are going to actually need because you need to find the BEST, and not just a warm body who has the right certifications.

Optimize Your Interviewing Skills

I suggest that you break your interviewing tasks into three parts. The first part is to simply talk with them on the phone. Ask about their reason for wanting to work in the center. Additional questions that are good to ask are:

Tell me about a time when you were presented with a challenge and how you overcame it? (if they have worked in a daycare before, then tailor that question to be more specific).

- What do you believe you will do when a parent comes to pick up a child and that child is crying?
- How would you handle two children, who are two years old, who begin fighting with one another?

- What would you say is your greatest strength when it comes to working with children?

- What are your plans for your own professional development and future?
- Can you commit to being with us for at least a year?
- What is your background in working with children?

Phase two of the interview process should be to have them take an online behavior assessment test. These tests are designed to uncover a person's underlying issues, if any, with discipline, children, and very often can uncover issues with drugs, lying, hostility, anger management or even drug use. This will further narrow down the candidate lists as some will just not want to be bothered to take the test, or they will be fearful of the test (in which case you definitely didn't want them).

The last phase is the actual face-to-face interview with those who have made the final cut. I would suggest that you NOT interview them alone. There are so many reasons for this, both legal and professional that I'm not going to list them out. Just believe me, you will want another pair of eyes and ears in the room. Plus, whomever you have assisting you can also help you in making final decisions.

Once you have a list of potential employees you still have some hoops to jump through. You will need to know that they have all of their licenses up to date as well as any required certifications. Last, but certainly not least, these teachers need to be caring, warm and loving, but also have a stable nature.

They need to have positive attitudes and get along with others. This is crucial not only because it makes them easier to get along with, but very young children are impressionable and will be influenced by the adults in their lives.

You want to provide the best possible role models for the children in your care. Good teachers are aware of that fact and are highly adept at being sensitive to a child's development, both physical, mental, emotional and cultural. The best teachers have all of those characteristics and they are highly organized.

Background Checks

This is required in nearly every state in the U.S. now, so you will need to have it done, not only to protect the children, but to protect your reputation. Most DMV offices can also run background checks, but there are also a number of online sources that can do the same thing. You will have to obtain permission from the candidate to do so. Expect to pay between $50-200 for these background checks. You are mainly looking to see if there are any red flags such as DUI charges, drug arrests or a criminal record.

Keeping Good Employees

Whole books have been devoted toward getting and keeping employees. The short version is to treat them right and with respect. Part of that is not just throwing them into the deep end of the pool and expecting them to swim. In other words you will need to develop an "onboarding" process, or an orientation for new caregivers and teachers.

New hires should go through a short orientation that should include the following:

- A tour of the facility.
- A discussion of the center's philosophy and its founding history.
- Meet with the other staff, especially the other teacher with whom he or she may be working.
- Special accommodations that must be made for some children.
- The planned activities and routine schedule.
- Discipline policies.
- Illness procedures (both for the new hire and for children who become ill).
- How meals, snack-time and naps are handled.
- Emergency procedures.
- Security procedures.
- General health policies, including taking children to the restroom, changing diapers, handling food in the kitchen, etc...
- Playground procedures.
- Sanitization policies.
- Curriculum.

Employee Files

You will be required to keep up to date files on everyone you hire. Here is a list of the must-haves:

- Current physical (this ensures that the teacher has no communicable diseases, has a T-DAP shot and a TB test on file)

- The most current background check and fingerprint check.

- Mandated Reporter Form (this is an agreement by the employee to report any suspected abuse of any of the children in their care)

- Discipline Agreement Form (shows that the employee was made aware of the discipline policies and agrees to follow them).

- A copy of the employees credentials and licensing.

- SIDS Training Certification (Sudden Infant Death Syndrome)

- Shaken Baby Syndrome Training Certification

- Food Handlers Training Certification

- Resume and letters of recommendation

- CPR and First Aid certificates

- W-4 and I-9 Forms

- Payroll Direct Deposit Form (if they want direct deposit)

Using Technology to Make Your Life Easier

As you can see, there's a lot to keep track of. Luckily there are a number of child care software companies out there who've designed software specifically for the purpose of keeping track of everything for you. The software can do everything from recordkeeping to billing, from attendance to tracking immunizations. Some of the most popular are:

- EZChildTrack Childcare Management Software
- ProCare
- Sandbox Child Care
- Childcare Sage
- Kinderlime

When assessing childcare management software programs make sure that they can handle all of the following:

- Scheduling and admissions.
- Enrollment.
- Billing and payment..
- Create reports for a number of categories.
- Handle and process payments.
- Track immunization for children.
- Alert administrators of children and staff birthdays.
- Check in and check out of staff.
- Payroll.
- Can send newsletters, texts, alerts or reports to parents.
- Meal planning and management.

Once you try an organizing software you will see that it is more than worth it. Most of the software is designed to automate most of the administrative tasks so you and your employees can focus on the children. Software comes in several platforms: cloud based and on-premises software. Most are also compatible with mobile devices.

Cloud Based Platforms

Cloud based platforms are usually offered as a subscription, billed monthly. The good news is that other than the initial subscription rate, there is no upfront investment. The company handles all of the updates and maintenance.

Premises Based Platforms

This is the type of management software that you buy, install and run on your own. There isn't a recurring monthly fee after the initial upfront payment, but that upfront payment can sometimes be quite high. If you need support or a tutorial you may pay extra.

Things to Think About

- How will you keep track of employees' training? Spreadsheet, paper files, both?

- Examine some of the software available for daycares, and see if any of them could work for you.

- Begin writing your own staff handbook.

- Get out a calendar and decide when you need to begin the task of finding teachers (well in advance of opening your doors).

- Be sure to visit my website to find "Employee Handbooks" and the online courses "How to find and Hire Quality Staff"

CHAPTER SEVEN
Getting the Word Out

When it comes to getting the word out about your daycare there are some options that are free, costing you nothing but time, and those that will cost you some money. When it comes to either types of marketing you will want to make sure that whether it's an investment of time or money, you get a good return. Keep in mind that marketing is much more than just advertising. It's also about building and maintaining relationships. It's about creating and building a unique market niche and then offering customers a way to view your center as having a perceived added value in comparison to other daycares in the area. For me, that was limiting the daycare to just boys with a focus on developing their inner character and foster a love for learning. For you, it might be something else. You need to figure what that "something else" is. Like with most things, it pays to make a list and have a strategy.

Create a Basic Marketing Plan

Marketing plans, sometimes called a business plan, have several sections, including an executive summary, your mission statement, marketing objectives, an analysis of your competitors as well as your target areas, and your action plan with budget considerations. The Childcare Aware foundation offers free marketing plan samples that you can look at to get a good idea of how to do yours. The bottom line, though, is to do one. If it seems like a lot of work….it is! But it is well worth it because at the end of it you will have a very clear idea of what your special "something" is that you can offer to families in the area.
Use the following quick outline to begin working on yours today.

Executive Summary

Write about who you are, why you wanted to start the business, the services you will offer, your target market, how you will know if you have been successful, and a quick overview of your marketing budget and ideas. This is actually best written after you've completed everything else and you have all of the information in front of you.

Mission Statement and Brand

This doesn't have to be very long. Just a few paragraphs about what your school will stand for and what your brand is. This is where you can decide what your logo will be. Include in this section what sets you apart from other centers.

Marketing Plan Objectives

What are your goals and how will you know you've achieved them? Your goals should be very specific in this section. For example, by the end of the first three months we will have enrolled 10 families and hired 4 teachers. We will have marketed to the community using magazines, local newspapers, social media and direct mail campaigns. We expect to have a response rate of at least 25%.

Market and Competitive Analysis

Who are the families in your area that you look to serve? Be specific. How many families live in your area. You can locate this information using the free data provided by the Census Bureau and local chamber of commerce. Include in this area the trends that are happening in the daycare business in your area and in the state. List all of your main competitors with their annual revenue listed (you can find this from reading their annual reports, usually posted online). What are your: strengths, weaknesses, opportunities and threats in the industry?

Marketing Strategy and Budget

Write about your logo, signage you will create, and the top 5 benefits you offer to parents who walk through your door. Are the prices you are offering competitive and consistent with the benefits you offer? What is the key message you want parents to take away with them. How much money do you have to put toward outreach?

Sample Cashflow Projections

This is the part where you will crunch numbers based on the number of children you realistically expect to have over the course of the next three years.

Marketing Strategies to Use

Once you have completed your marketing plan you'll need to focus specifically on how you want to get the word out. For me it was kinda simple; I already had a forum and a way to get publicity. I realize that this not what's available to most of you, but understand that even though I used my celebrity to get started, I still had to do marketing just like anyone else. Use the following ideas to let people know about your business.

Strategy One: Create an outstanding logo. Hire a graphic artist to professional render a logo for your center. Use this on everything from business cards to fliers. The average cost for this can run from $500-750.

Strategy Two: Create a website. It might be tempting to use one of those quick-build sites that you see advertised on TV, but believe me you'll just end up hiring someone else down the road. Cut to the chase from the start and pay someone to build the website and maintain it for you. The average cost for this is $650-1,200 (or more depending on what features you'd like). Submit your website to all of the major search engines and list your center on all online daycare directories. To find those directories put in the keyword: daycare directory and you'll get a massive list.

Strategy Three: Print brochures and fliers. Aim for 250 and 500 for each. Vistaprint offers very reasonable pricing for this, but shop around. It can run you from $100 to $400 depending on what you want done.

Strategy Four: Place fliers in various places where you know families frequent. That could be indoor play centers, toy stores, parks, libraries, book stores, ice cream shops and grocery stores. Just anywhere you know families will show up. Make sure to ask permission before you start putting them up, though. Aside from the cost of the fliers, this costs you nothing but time.

Strategy Five: Plan to have an outreach event in the community. Find out when there are going to be some local events, set up a table and hand out fliers. Offer a book exchange, where parents bring a book, and take a book. Costs you nothing but your time.

Strategy Six: Place an ad in the local parents' magazine or newspaper. Typical cost is $250 per ad (this may vary depending on your publications).

Strategy Seven: Create social media pages. At least have a Twitter, Facebook and Instagram account. These allow you to post fun activities your students, parents and teachers experience in the center. It also allows you to quickly notify and education parents to various aspects of the center as well as caring for their child. Cost is free to set up social media unless you have someone do it for you.

Strategy Eight: Record a greeting on the answering machine/voicemail that gives those leaving a message important information about the center's benefits.

Strategy Nine: Network. Join a business organization, such as the chamber of commerce or other business association. Speaking with other business people can give you ideas for how to better your own.

Strategy Ten: Attend as many SBA (Small Business Administration) workshops as you can. Each one gives you more insight into the business side of running a daycare. And, you will also meet others whom you can tell about your center. Who knows…maybe they have a child.

Strategy Eleven: Google Adwords. Hire someone to create an Adword campaign and run it for you for a few months. If it is done correctly every time someone from your area types in keywords related to daycare or childcare, your Google Ad will show up. The cost is approximately $5 a day, as a basic rate.

Strategy Twelve: Word of mouth is golden. Don't discount the power of a good review on such places as Yelp! Or Google reviews. If you have happy parents, ask them to help you out and place a review for you online. One center I know offered to enter participating parents' names into a raffle for a nice prize, just for taking the time to write the review.

Your Center's Sign

There are a couple of signs that you can have made that will attract attention and let those in the community know that you are opening your doors. The first type are lawn signs. You wouldn't think they would be very successful, but they are surprisingly effective. Plus, aside from the cost of the signs, they are free to post. Buildasign.com offers a very reasonable price on those. Just make sure you don't clutter the sign with too many pictures and that you make it easily readable by people who are driving by.

The other type of sign is one that is more permanent. It will depend on the type of building you have. If the building you are in already has a space allocated for a sign, then you can simply find a sign company in your area and have them create one for you. If you don't have a designated space, then you will need to consider what type of sign you'd like to have. You can get a sign like you see at most elementary schools where there is a large space in the middle for you to place letters in it to act as another means of communicating important information. You can also get a sign that remains static, has your logo on it and the name of your center. These types of signs are usually located near the entrance or the main roadway.

Things to Think About

- Make a checklist of types of advertising you'd like to try.

- Locate your local SBA and plan to attend a workshop or schedule a time to speak with an agent.

- Find someone to make a website for you, and get a graphic designer to professionally create fliers, business cards and brochures.

- Find a simple business plan through the SBA website and create yours.

- Be sure to visit my website to sign up for the online course "How to Market your Daycare on a Budget" **www.coreyparchman.com**

CHAPTER EIGHT
The Parent Handbook

Developing a handbook with all of your policies and procedures explained can head off a lot of headache and misunderstanding down the road. When parents have an easy reference where they can see what your policies are regarding a sick child, missed days or payment policies, then it will save everyone time and trouble. Visit my website for a edited version of my Parent Handbook. There are some critical parts that have to be put in there, believe me, or you will end up having to go back in after you open up.

Structure of a Parent Handbook

The cover should have your logo on it and the name of the school, along with the name of the director. Plan to bind these handbooks with some type of binder. A plastic spiral binding is nice.

Letter from the Owner

This should be a short letter of welcome from the owner. List why you opened your doors, what you like to see happening in the center and what the benefits are of selecting your center.

Staff Directory

In the early pages there should be a listing of all the teachers, their credentials, and phone numbers, if applicable. It should also list the main number for the center, and the direct line to the director. Some centers put a picture of the teachers next to these, but this can cause a problem if you have a teacher that leaves, but their picture and information is still there.

Code of Ethics Statement

This is different from your mission statement that you wrote in the business plan. Most daycares simply utilize the NAEYC code of ethical standards from their website. It is free to copy.

Mission Statement

This is where your personal philosophy about learning and working with children is written.

Hours of Operation and Calendar

Does your center follow the public school year calendar, or something different? Are you open traditional work hours (9-5), or later. Do you offer a drop off service, part time enrollment, or offer nontraditional hours that go later than and earlier than the 9-5? How is drop off handled and what are the expectations? Make sure that you have parents indicate who is to drop off and pickup their child.

Required Forms for Enrollment

This could be a simple checklist of what you need from them in order to enroll their child. Forms could include the registration form, emergency contact card, physicals and immunization reports.

Curriculum Explained

You will need to explain what type of curriculum you are using and why. Make sure to list out objectives and goals that each age's curriculum hopes to achieve.

Discipline Policy Explained

This is a very important section as it will communicate with the parents what the center's philosophy is for administering discipline when needed. Most centers use a time out and a series of steps before a child is asked to leave the center because of behavioral problems.

Billing and Payments

You will need to be very specific in how you word this section so that parents do not misunderstand what they are being charged, when the payment is due, what happens if the payment is late, and what a parent can do if he or she is no longer able to afford childcare (there are some services that can subsidize their payments). This is where you can also offer recurring automatic payments (for a discount), or spell out under what terms you will accept certain forms of payment. Do you offer credits or partial refunds? You will also need to determine at which point a family will no longer be offered service due to non-payment.

Food Service

If you offer a food service at the center, then you will need to spell out what the policies are for delivering meals. However you decide to do it, make sure it is clear in this part of the handbook.

Health Policies

Children will get sick, as will staff. This section of the handbook needs to spell out under what circumstances they should keep their sick child at home. Most centers go with the fever rule. If the child is running a fever then he or she must stay home. This is true for employees as well. Spell out what arrangements are made if a child comes to school and becomes ill, or comes to school and is ill.

Parent Involvement and Communication

In this section you will want to outline the expectations you have when it comes to parental behavior and involvement in their child's activities at the school. It is also a good section to place means of communication and how your center keeps in contact with them on a regular basis. This could be via a regular newsletter, through the parent portal on your website, via texts, or all of the above.

Emergency Preparedness

This is the section where you will let parents know in the event of inclement weather or long term power outages what your procedure will be for handling them. On such days what types of transportation or accommodation will be provided for children at the center?

Accreditation and Licensing Information

Parents will want to know that your center is fully licensed, insured and accredited in accordance with your state's rules. This is the section where you list your licensing numbers, and insurance. List the accrediting agency and the ranking you received. List inspections that are regularly scheduled throughout the year and your track record thus far.

Grievance Policy

Hopefully you will never need to exercise this policy, but if a parent has a problem with you, staff or the center, then he or she needs to know how to go about making their concerns known. Having a dedicated way for parents to speak with you can go a long way toward causing any further upset. Usually this is simply a quick reminder that if there are any problems they can make an appointment to speak directly with the director and the teacher together. Never allow a parent and teacher to speak alone with one another, even if it is in a conference room on the premises. There are too many ways that could go sideways. Keep in mind that for each state there are certain sections that are required to be included. Each state's requirements can be found through the Child Care Aware site.

Things to Think About

- Read through a sample Parents Handbook. Circle those areas that you like best and rewrite them for your parents handbook. Do NOT copy it straight out.
- Visit my website for a copy of my Parent Handbook. www.coreyparchman.com

CHAPTER NINE
The Staff Handbook

As you first start out you may not think that there is any need for an actual staff handbook. Don't make that assumption or that mistake. A staff handbook is crucial to communicate the mission and purpose of your program, to lay out in black and white what you expect from those who work in your center, and it can be a valuable resource for your staff. Having a staff book can make sure that your team is on the same path and if they have questions, they know to look in the handbook first to find the answers.

Beyond that, the staff handbook helps you to maintain a quality standard, a level of care that you can point to in concrete terms. I would suggest that even if you area three man operation you go ahead and create the staff book as if you have at least a dozen people working with you. Because, hey, at some point you might and you'll already have the handbook expanded to cover more than just the basics of job descriptions and privacy rules.

What you include in a daycare staff handbook is completely up to you. I'm offering you a look into the basic sections that can be included. Use the following information to construct your own. There are numerous sections that can be included, and depending on what your state's requirements are, some of them will absolutely have to be in your handbook. Some of the sections you will most definitely want to include are the employment requirements, job descriptions, salary scales and your policy for missed days and tardiness. Most states require you place a non-discrimination policy clearly in writing as well as a sexual harassment policy.

Sections regarding procedures in dealing with very young children should also be outlined. The following will delve briefly into all of the various sections for you to consider. If you'd like to see a completed one, ChildCare Aware and NAEYC have samples.

Opening Pages

Just as with the Parent's Handbook, include a welcome letter from the director and a table of contents so that staff can easily refer back to the sections they need throughout the course of their employment with you. The other opening pages should also include your mission statement, your Quality Care Standards (credentials you have and the daycare has…such as accreditation, licensing, etc…). Some directors also like to include the business's history or something about the owner of the center and why he or she decided to take the leap into daycare. For me it was reaching out to a group of kids that I thought needed a little extra attention in an area where kids are mostly overlooked. For you, the story may be a different one. Don't be afraid to share that.

Employment Pages

This section should match your state's hiring regulations for daycare and daycare workers. This is the section where you include information about how you hire, what you expect, and your non-discrimination and sexual harassment policies. It is also helpful to create a type of organizational chart to show the chain of command so that new hires can quickly understand who they should go to if they have a problem. This is where the delegation of responsibilities can be spelled out. Also make sure to include the background check, fingerprinting and regulations required by your state when hiring someone to work with children.

Program Pages

Use this space to discuss the type of curriculum that you use and how you expect teachers to use it. Outline the basic name of the book, why you selected it and what the overall curriculum's goal is for each age range. In this section make sure you outline how you have special accommodations for children with special needs or those overcoming specific challenges. A small section explaining your confidentiality and privacy rules should also be included. Sensitive information should always be kept out of the public area of the center, and certainly not outside the center.

General Policies and Typical Schedules

You can reuse some of the material from the Parent's handbook in this section as it should show new hires what your typical schedule is like, what the lead teachers and assistant teachers are responsible for, how you deal with taking the children outdoors and how field trips are handled.

If your center provides a meal, then those procedures should be outlined. However, if children bring their own lunches to school, then mealtime procedures for storing food and retrieving lunchboxes must be discussed. Children who are very young and still require diapering will have very specific requirements and regulations. Procedures for taking children to the toilet must also be followed. A complete step by step poster has been created by the CCR&R that you can print out and post as a reminder.

Outline exactly how you handle nap time, and what the procedure is. For example, some centers have done away with back rubbing as children fall asleep, while others have parents sign a permission form giving caregivers permission to offer comfort while a child goes to sleep. Will your center allow a child to bring their security blanket, a favorite toy to nap with? Do you have a back-to-sleep policy, or are there provisions for removing and supervising children who are not able to nap?

This section should also include a some information about using materials, toys and equipment in the center. Are toys and materials rotated each month, each week? How often do you expect teachers to change these out? Cover the sanitization of these toys and how that is accomplished. Do lead teachers create a wish list of items they would like to have in the classroom? Is each teacher given a budget and allowed to select child appropriate toys, or is this left to the director?

Discuss any regularly recurring staff meetings. I recommend you opt for at least one meeting a month so that you can give everyone a chance to ask questions and so you can bring them up to date on any changes or expectations that need to be met. You should make it clear that these meetings, which will have to be held when there are no children at the center, is mandatory. We like to order take out, or do pot luck and everyone eat and chat. It can be a great team building event, too.

Lastly, focus on the level of supervision that is expected by the employee in all areas of the center, from their classrooms to the outdoor play area to the meal room to the bathroom. Everything should be addressed so there is no confusion at all.

Employee Behavior

If you leave out sections, don't leave this section out. This is where you spell out how you expect your staff to dress. Be specific as regards clothing, shoes and jewelry. If you will have your employees wearing nametags, address how this should be worn and when it should be worn. Though it should be obvious, make sure to mention that there is no designated smoking area in a childcare center.

Most centers, for good reason, have a no-eating policy for teachers. Food employees bring from home may not be consumed in front of the children while in class. If your center offers a meal, then the teacher should eat the same food as the children, if possible, acting as a role model for healthy eating habits. Staff should avoid drinking hot beverages around children since there is the possibility of burns occurring. Those with safety lids may be okay, but you will have to determine what you will allow. If employees have medication that they need to take during the day, make sure the teacher is aware that the medication needs to be stored out of reach and sight of children.

Some centers allow the use of a television or videos in the classroom but you should be clear how often and for how long you allow television to be watched. Talk radio or adult radio shows or music should not be allowed in a daycare classroom.

Personal phone calls and cell phone use, including texting, should also be discussed. Will you allow staff to freely interact using text throughout the day, or do you have a zero tolerance for this as long as they are actively on the clock?

Do you have a provision for sick days? How are those handled? If an employee needs time off how do they go about requesting this? Make sure the procedure for doing so is completely outlined. If an employee calls in sick are they responsible for finding their own substitute? How much advanced notice do you require?

Discuss payroll and how/when paychecks are issued. If you offer direct deposit, include the form for the information. Make sure employees understand that you will need them to submit the proper forms for withholding. Also discuss any benefits that the center offers.

Include a section about orientation. Most states require that there be at least 10-16 hours of orientation for new hires. Go through the basic progression of orientation. Also include a specific list of circumstances that will lead to their immediate dismissal. This can include anything from allowing a child to leave with someone who is not authorized to neglecting or abusing a child. Include a grievance process and how conflict is handled and resolved at your center.

Lastly, include a section outlining what everyone is expected to do in the case of an emergency situation. What does the teacher do when a child has a serious accident? What are the plans for evacuation in the event of a fire, flood, tornado or other natural event? Discuss health policies and medication policies. At the very end of the handbook make sure you have a space for the new employee to sign and date, as well as a place for the director to sign and date. This covers you in case the employee comes back and says they were not informed of a policy. By signing the form they indicate that they have read and agreed to the rules stated in the handbook.

It may seem like a lot of work, but there are a number of templates out on the net for you to use. The bottom line is to make sure you have covered as many bases as you are required to, and then cover those that you feel are very important. Making sure you have clearly stated how you expect your employees to act and to which codes of conduct you will hold them accountable for is crucial to running your center like a well oiled machine.

Things to Think About

- Locate and print out several samples of staff handbooks from daycare and daycare centers. Notice how they put together their different areas, then using that as a guideline, construct your own.
- Make sure that the language you use is not too full of legal jargon and that it is easy to understand.
- Visit my website for a copy of my Staff Handbook. www.coreyparchman.com

CHAPTER TEN
Selecting Curriculum

Whether you plan to offer a daycare, or whether you will include a daycare with a daycare, most parents will expect you to provide more than a babysitting service. They want you to offer their children a way to grown both emotionally and mentally. Quality programs can't help but stand out from those around them. That's in part what happened with me. All I was focused on, initially, was providing a way for young daycare boys to receive additional direction and support in their most formative years. But, as a result of that in a very short time we started to stand out. Not only were we attracting attention for the service we were providing to an underserved demographic, but we were also offering a super high quality academic program. A lot of that has to do with our curriculum. Yours should too.

I know that there's not always a lot of spare money to put down on loads of curriculum right off the bat. So that's why you need to make the money you do spend worth it. One of the first things you have to do is to prioritize learning time. That doesn't mean that you literally schedule every minute of the children's time there, not allowing for any playtime, but rather you create educational plans that work for all age groups. The best curriculum can be scaled up for older ages and scaled down for younger children.

Don't discount the value of playtime. Even Mr. Rogers was a fan of it because it gives kids a chance to work on their social interactions with one another, build teambuilding skills and enjoy being active.

Curriculum doesn't have to come with a lot of bells and whistles, either. At its core it should focus on basic skills, emphasizing numbers, letters, alphabet learning, shapes, colors and being able to count in chronological order, to name a few.

Types of Curriculum

Curriculum developed for the very young child are created in one of two ways: Research Based Curriculum and Curriculum Scope and Sequence. Both are quite good. Here's the differences between the two.

Research Based Curriculum

This type of curriculum is based on the most current early childhood research at the time. It is based on new discoveries on how children learn and develop. Usually it is very content-rich and focuses on specific types of instruction that are developmentally appropriate.

Curriculum Scope and Sequence

Curriculum Scope and Sequence also uses prevailing theories but also incorporates successful theories of the past that have not be disputed. Scope and sequence offers an organized procedure for initiating learning and reaching the educational objective. These are often the easiest to scale up or scale down.

What Should You Look for in Curriculum

Specifically, you want to find a curriculum that engages the children in several areas: cognitively, language development, social, emotional, physical and cultural.

When we talk about cognitive, that's what most people think about when they think about a school. It's the numbers, shapes, patterns, art, music, counting, measurements, experience with the world around them and dramatic play. Language development is one of the more crucial areas for children because they are not often able to communicate what is going on inside their minds because they lack the words to do that. Teaching children how to communicate, which includes both listening and speaking, understanding the sounds that letters make and the patterns in language, are all critically important. Learning to love literature and reading, and being read to, can form a very strong bond between young children and language skills.

Children also need to learn how to interact with one another in a positive way. A good curriculum will include this as well as opportunities for children to show respect for themselves and others. This also follows closely along with emotional intelligence, being able to recognize and identify basic emotions, learn useful life skills for self-control, and learning to develop empathy for others.

Curriculum should also give children a chance to learn about their bodies and the physical world around them. Active play, directed play that is a part of the curriculum can help children to learn about healthy habits, and develop a desire to live an active lifestyle as adults.

Last, but definitely not least, a curriculum should offer children a chance to learn about and express their awareness for their own, and others', culture. Providing a foundation for tolerance, understanding, curiosity and appreciation for a culture not like their own may very well change the course of our society.

Assessing a Potential Curriculum Series

If you are planning to offer a Head Start program at your school, there are very strict performance standards that have to be met by your curriculum. The curriculum is often referred to as ELDS or Early Learning Development Standards. A document outlining what these are specifically is available on the [Head Start site](#), but the general highlights include making sure that the curriculum you use hits all of the areas of learning for children. In order for a curriculum to be effective it has to provide content that is not only academically enriching but is meaningful and interesting to children. Head Start requires that the following domains be addressed by the curriculum you choose:

- Social and Emotional Development
- Approaches to Learning
- Language and Literacy
- Perceptual, Motor and Physical Development
- Cognition

Good Curriculum to Use

Little Treasures

This curriculum is created by the academic powerhouse of Macmillan/McGraw-Hill, who create textbooks for use in elementary, middle and high schools, too. Their Little Treasures curriculum is laid out in units and follows themes. Resources for activities, materials lists, books to read with extensions, and modifications for children who have developmental delays are included. There are printables that are available for free to use along with the curriculum. Each unit in this series hits each of the recommended domains listed above.

HighScope

HighScope is very popular and is very successful in areas where children have been identified as "at risk". Several studies have been done that have tracked children for several decades and have found the children who participated in this type of curriculum tended to graduate from high school at higher rates, as well as live in lower crime neighborhoods. The HighScope curriculum focuses on decision making, creativity, cooperation, independence and problem solving. Many daycares use this in combination with another curriculum so that all of the domains are addressed.

Creative Curriculum

This is a research based curriculum and is ideally situated to be scaled up or down for numerous age ranges. This is a very good curriculum for both center based and home based daycares. Creative Curriculum was developed in perfect alignment with Head Start guidelines and framework. One of the key components with this series is goal setting and recognizing achievements when accomplished.

Additional Curriculum to Explore:
- Core Knowledge® Daycare
- Sequence
- Curiosity Corner
- Frog Street Pre-K
- DLM Early Childhood Express®
- HighReach Learning®
- Innovations: The

- Comprehensive Daycare
- Curriculum
- The InvestiGator Club®
- Opening the World of Learning
- (OWL)
- Let's Begin with the Letter
- People®
- DaycareFirst
- Tools of the Mind
- Scholastic Big Day for PreK™

The National Center on Quality Teaching and Learning has reviewed all of these curriculum so you can go and decide when may be worth your investment. Keep in mind that the curriculum will form one of the major backbones and structure for your daycare so this is not a choice that should be taken lightly. Take your time, read through a number of them, then order a sample so that you can look at them closely.

Things to Think About

- Plan to review and compare at least five different types of curriculum before making your decision.
- Talk with teachers and staff, if possible, and get their input.
- What are other centers using successfully?
- Look through online forums and LinkIn groups to see what other directors think about various curriculum.

CHAPTER ELEVEN

Accreditation

Unlike public schools, accreditation is voluntary for privately owned schools, daycares and daycares. However, accreditation means that your school has met a high standard for social, academic and quality programming and standards. There are a number of legit accreditation organizations, each with their own process toward accreditation. One of the most popular is the NAEYC's accreditation process, which is what I'll talk about below. But, I'll also list the other accreditation organizations so you can choose the one that works the best for you. Getting accredited is something you want to do because it not only legitimizes your center, but it lets parents know that you offer a high standard of care and programming, which will translate into higher tuition rates and profit margins. It is a win/win situation. The steps to accreditation below are the NAEYC process, but in general, most accrediting organization follow something similar. So, if you prepare the following items and processes, you'll be set for anything the others may throw at you.

Steps to Accreditation

Most accrediting organizations have a three or four step process. The first one is a self-assessment that you will complete, and a second assessment that is completed by the accrediting organization. This involves school visits, discussions with the teachers, and assessment of the curriculum and classroom observation. Based on this assessment, the inspector will give approval for accreditation, or will recommend improvements. Almost everyone has to improve in some areas, so don't get upset if you don't pass the first time around. Only about 10% are accredited by NAEYC each year (GreatSchools has a good site that gives you the stats).

What Will Be Assessed?

The assessor will visit several times to make his or her determination about the school. He or she will evaluate the center based on relationships of staff and with children and parents, the curriculum, teaching methods and strategies, how children's progress is monitored and recorded, health and safety, teachers' credentials, community relationships, the physical environment and adherence to state laws, and even you as the director will be assessed. Some inspectors ask to have parent interviews, so have a few parents in mind who would be good interview prospects. Reach out to those parents to make sure they are willing to help.

Accreditation Recommendation

It might not feel like it at the time, but the inspectors really do want you do succeed. He or she will make recommendations and suggestions as the process moves forward. While you may be meeting state standards, most accreditation requires you to not only meet, but exceed those standards in some areas. Accreditation is not the same as being fully licensed, though they are often confused.

Your licensing is your license to do business in the county/state where you are located. So, while all daycares and daycares have to be licensed, not all of them are accredited. If your daycare is going to be run through a church, then they are often exempt from the accreditation recommendations.

Other Accrediting Programs Besides NAEYC

- American Montessori Society (AMS)
- Accredited Professional Daycare Learning Environment (APPLE)
- National Early Childhood Program Accreditation (NECPA)

Getting Help: Accreditation Facilitators

If you've never gone through accreditation before, then it can be worth it to get some help from an Accreditation Facilitation Project consultant (AFP). These AFP personnel understand all of the requirements of the accreditation process and will give you personalized direction. Technical assistance, support, and advice on this level can often fast track the accreditation process because it cuts down on the trial and error nature of the assessment and evaluation process. To find someone near you, you can access the AFP Directory.

What Will it Cost?

These prices are current as of 2018 and are those listed for NAEYC. Each accrediting association has their own set fees. But, this can give you a ballpark idea of what it may cost you. Basically, it is built around the number of children you have in your center. When you first start out you should focus on things like running the center and solidifying your schedule and framework. But, as soon as possible, consider getting that accreditation as it can leapfrog your marketing and outreach efforts. Once accredited it is good for 5 years and the renewal fees are much less.

Number of Children	Accreditation Phase	Total Fee Initially	Renewal Fee
Less than 60	Pursuing Accreditation	$1,570	$550
61-120	Pursuing Accreditation	$1,945	$650
121-240	Pursuing Accreditation	$2,420	$775
241-360	Pursuing Accreditation	$2,795	$885

Safety Guidelines

One of the big areas where you'll be evaluated is on the overall safety of your center. This includes drop off and pick up procedures as well as how the staff interact with the children, how discipline is dealt with, as well as the overall safety of the building and equipment. There is an actual checklist that you can use to evaluate all of these areas. Almost a 100 different areas and zones are considered in the overall safety of your program, staff, environment and center.

Things to Think About

- Get the inspection checklist for accreditation from the NAEYC website.
- List the improvements you can make in the short term, mid-term, and long term. Set specific months and years for accomplishing them.
- Use the safety checklist provided above. How well are you meeting those? Where do you need to make improvements?

CHAPTER TWELVE

Setting a Sustainable Pricing Structure

I would love to tell you that I got this part right, right off the bat, but to tell you the truth, it took me many months of tweaking things to come to the right operating capital to keep things running well. Set your prices too low and you might find yourself with more month than money when it comes to keeping the lights on. Charge too much and you may price yourself too high above the competition. So, how do you get to that Goldilocks zone for pricing and structure? I don't claim to have all of the answers, but here's what worked for me.

Snoop

What are other centers in your area charging? You'll need to determine what they charge per age of the child, whether the child is full time, part time, drop ins, and if there is an initial registration fee. All of these can add to, or take away from, your bottom line. Things you'll need to keep in mind are how much of a profit you want to make, what the average salary is of families in your area, and what agencies exist in your area to help struggling families meet childcare and daycare costs. The rule of thumb is that families can usually afford to pay at least 10 percent of their annual salaries on tuition.

Daycares will charge more than daycares because they offer a structured curriculum and not just a babysitting service. This justifies setting the fee structure like a private school would. Most daycares charge an enrollment fee that is approximately half of what the child's tuition would be. This covers you for all of the extra paperwork and data entry that has to happen in order for you to create an account for that child and his/her family.

Setting Your Fees

How much you charge will depend on how much you spend and what you want your profit to be once everyone has taken their cut each month.

- How much do you spend on payroll? (What is the going per hour rate for teachers and staff?)
- How much do you spend on materials and supplies?
- What's it cost to keep the lights on?
- What do you want your profit to be?
- How many children can your current space accommodate based on your state standards?
- What types of taxes are you expected to pay?

A Basic Example

Consider the case of a child that attends full time as a three year old. There's a six to one requirement for teacher to child ratios, so if the labor cost is $13 an hour (which includes withholding and benefits), then each child needs to be charged $2.17 per hour. Then, the materials cost needs to be added in. That average is $5.85 per child, per day. Overhead costs to run the business can be estimated at about 30% of your labor and materials cost. A good net profit is between nine to 14 percent of the gross receipts. So, the price breakdown given all of this is approximately this:

- $104 per day, per teacher. (assuming an 8 hour work day)
- $104.16 for six children (at capacity), or $17.36 per day, per child.
- $175 for materials for the week, or $35 for the classroom each day.
- $83.70 for overhead to run that one classroom.

You are looking at about $800.00 just to run that one classroom for a week and that is without any profit to you. With only $520.80 in income that classroom is not paying for itself. So, as the director you'd have to adjust something somewhere. Many directors charge more for younger children because they require more direct focused attention. Some may not be fully potty trained, or will still have accidents throughout the day. Most centers will charge at least 20 percent more for younger children. In the above scenario that increases the charge to a little over $20 a day per child. However, that is still not going to get you to any kind of a profit margin.

Now consider that the average salary of the parents living in your area is approximately $52,000 a year for a single head of household, and $81,000 for a couple. Based on these numbers, a single head of household could afford $5,200 per year on tuition, and a two parent family could afford $8,100 per year. Break that down further, and you'd find that a single would be about $433 a month, or $108.30 per week, and that is approximately $21 a day. Doubles could pay $675 a month, $168.75 a week, and $33.75 a day. Based on that, you could begin charging $27 per day for four and five year olds, and those older three year olds who were potty trained. Younger children could be charged a few dollars more. In this scenario, you would be making $4,050 per month for that classroom. Minus expenses you are looking at approximately $900 profit on each classroom per month, assuming it is operating at full capacity. Based on that you can calculate how many classrooms you'd need to have in order to meet your own salary requirements. As you can see, working backwards from the annual salary in an area is the better way to estimate your costs.

Should You Charge by the Hour?

Obviously, if you offer a drop-in service as a sort of daycare/babysitting service, then charging by the hour makes sense. However, charging by the hour for daycare just isn't practical. Plus, children need to be there every day to receive the full benefit of the educational hours.

Other Charges to Consider

Sometimes employers are not concerned with their workers' childcare and daycare concerns and will ask them to come in early or work later than the daycare's usual hours. How will you handle that? Many charge an overtime fee, which is time and a half of the usual charge. Also consider charging the enrollment fee, and even a small materials fee depending on the age of your child. Some centers also charge for having to launder children's clothing that become soiled during the course of the day.

Billing and Invoicing

As discussed in an earlier chapter, there are a number of software programs that will make the invoicing and billing less of a headache. But, those programs can be expensive when you are first starting out. You may just opt to do it yourself for a bit to see if you really want to go that route. If so, consider doing the following to make your life easier.

Offer Convenience

Parents of young children are hopelessly busy and it's easy for them to forget to take care of sending out the payment on time…even if you've put numerous signs up and sent home reminders. Make it easy for them to pay you by offering the option to pay online. Most parents have a credit card or debit care on hand and can make a quick payment online in a few minutes. You can also set up an automatic withdrawal option with the parents' bank account.

Many centers offer a discount for parents who will use the automatic withdrawal system. There's also fees you can charge for late payments, returned checks, and so forth. If you want to offer online billing you'll need to have an account set up with some sort of service. Paypal, Square or other similar types of services are cheap to set up and use, initially. Most of those can be integrated into your existing website.

Be Consistent With the Rules

Believe me, once you bend the rules for one, you'll find yourself bending it for everyone and then you're in a mess. Let them know it's not personal but remain firm. Always make the due date the same each month, and make sure that if a pay date falls on a weekend, that you let parents know when the due date actually is.
Some centers create a billing schedule that parents can put on their 'fridge. You'll thank me for that advice.

Keep to a Billing Schedule

Keep the billing schedule simple, the invoice straightforward and send it out at exactly the same time each month. You might be tempted to send a billing statement out each week requiring payment, but this is going to cause a paperwork nightmare. Tracking something like that is going to make you reach for the TUMS like candy.

Send Reminders and Post Notices

Putting up signs in the center, sending home a reminder in the newsletter, putting the payment reminder on the website, send an email or text blast, and advertising pay dates on the signs near the parking lot are all good ways to remind parents that payment is going to be due. Put those notices up well in advance so they have time to get to it.

Getting Parents Payment Assistance

Each state has their own set of government and local agencies that can help parents afford childcare and daycare. Research what some of those are in your area and make sure to list that in the parents' handbook. In most instances, parents who want their child to attend your school can find assistance if they truly need it. Government agencies will cut you a check each month for their portion of the tuition, and the parents are responsible for paying their portion. Each subsidy organization handles it a bit differently, but in general, that's how it is split and paid. If you have parents receiving assistance then they will need to sign a form for you that allows you to directly speak with the casework to check the status of the authorization and what the parents' amount is. Keep in mind that most government agencies can take at least 30-60 days to pay you, but the parents can still pay their part on time.

Things to Think About

- Find out what the average salary is for your area, then calculate what you should charge per child, per age group.

- How many classrooms will you need to run in order to make the profit margin you are hoping for?

- Locate the nearest Child Care Referral Agency and speak to them about subsidies for low income parents.

- Decide how you will bill, invoicing policies and fees.

- Speak with your Web Developer to see if he or she can add in the payment portal for parents.

- Determine how you'll remind parents.

www.coreyparchman.com

ABOUT THE AUTHOR

Corey Parchman is the Founder of two very successful daycare franchises. Mini Men Pre K Leadership Academy and Pre K University Corey was born and raised in Indianapolis, Indiana, is the youngest of 3 children by Vivian Parchman and the late Edward Parchman who passed away when Corey was 9 years old. Corey attended Indianapolis Public Schools and graduated from Manual High School where he excelled in sports.

In track, Corey was:
- 100 meter dash City Champ
- 100 meter dash Conference Champ
- Two time Long Jump Sectional and Regional Champ
- Two time 100 meter dash Sectional and Regional Champ.
- Two time 200 meter dash Sectional and Regional Champ

In football, as a quarterback, he was:
- Two time All City, First Team
- Two time All Conference First Team
- All State
- All Metro
- District 7 All Star

Corey also was the starting quarterback for the South in the Annual Indiana North South All Star Football Classic.

After high school Corey accepted a football scholarship to Ball State University. Corey earned a Bachelor's degree in Elementary Education and a Minor in Human Relations. Corey was a standout athlete while at Ball State and was once known as the fastest player in college football. He holds several records at Ball State including highest kick return average in a season and in a career, most kick return yards in a season, career and a game. Corey also holds a Ball State and NCAA Football record for longest kick return (105 yards) in a game, which is still a record today. Because of this record breaking feat, he was featured on CBS' Late Show with David Letterman. After college, Corey was selected by the NFL Jacksonville Jaguars as an Undrafted Free Agent. He spent time with several NFL teams throughout his career including the Jacksonville Jaguars, Indianapolis Colts, St. Louis Rams, Oakland Raiders and the Green Bay Packers. After retiring from the NFL, Corey pursued a career in business. He is the current owner and founder of several successful endeavors including: Mini Men Pre K Academy, Pre K University Academy, Parchman Development, Clear Vision Media, Executive Concierge and Core Par Enterprise. Corey is also an educator and philanthropist.

Made in the USA
Coppell, TX
27 June 2024

34000692R00049